TIME

INSIDE

❖

TIME

INSIDE

Gary Margolis

GREEN WRITERS PRESS *Brattleboro, Vermont*

Printed in the United States

10 9 8 7 6 5 4 3 2

Green Writers Press is a Vermont-based publisher whose mission
is to spread a message of hope and renewal through the words and
images we publish. Throughout, we will adhere to our commitment
to preserving and protecting the natural resources of the earth. To that
end, a percentage of our proceeds will be donated to environmental
activist groups. Green Writers Press gratefully acknowledges support
from individual donors, friends, and readers to help support the
environment and our publishing initiative.

Giving Voice to Writers Who Will Make the World a Better Place
Green Writers Press | Brattleboro, Vermont
www.greenwriterspress.com

ISBN: 978-1-7320815-5-0

COVER PHOTO BY IGOR STEVANOVIC - DREAMSTIME.COM

Acknowledgments

The author gratefully acknowledges first appearance of the poems in the following periodicals, sometimes in earlier versions.

Addison Independent: "On the Lift," "November Street"

Roads Taken: Contemporary Vermont Poetry: "Chagall's Girl," "Runner Without a Number"

Vermont Public Radio Downton Abbey Gala Program: "Downton's Last Lawn"

My gratitude to Ratang Sedimo, Middlebury College student, for his technical expertise in front cover design. (*Porta dos ceus, Heaven's Door*, Igor Stevanovic, 1989, DREAMSTIME.)

To my friend, Richard Hawley, for suggesting the title for this book.

And to the inmates, correctional officers and volunteer services, affording me the opportunity to facilitate a poetry writing program in their maximum security facility.

Notes

Correction officer: CO

"Welcoming You to the Counseling Center" ~ for Donna Scheuring Stark, on the occasion of her retirement from Middlebury College.

"Visiting Poet" ~ for the Midland School, Los Olivos, California.

For my sister, Shelley.
(1949–2018)

For the men and women inside.

CONTENTS

1

2

3

4

5

6

I MAKE A TREE INSIDE MY CELL

and hang some paper bells I cut
from memory. The angel I have
to believe is inside me.

Even with men raving
on my block, using a kind
of gangster, reindeer talk.

I give myself everything
I can receive. Nothing
that could pass through

a metal memory. Randomly
I guess today will be my day
to be stripped-searched. To have

my cell tree-tossed. So the bells
can think they're ringing
for me and the angel on my block.

Dressed in snowing, everyday green.
I make a manger in my cell,
my paper room. And light a match

to bring the wise men in. To celebrate
my loneliness. To see a ribbon's
fuming smoke.

APPLYING TO VOLUNTEER

In the third stanza you'll hear
your fingerprints rejected.
Ink doesn't like smooth skin,

citizens who want to
volunteer. No matter how many
times you're told to go home

and return, to scrape your hands.
So the ink will take.
A poem doesn't know how many lines

it takes to do its work, to be taken in.
In an inmate's heart.
It can take a lifetime to write

a sentence in a cellblock.
You're told, in volunteer training,
once you're inside, not to look

down, to gaze straight ahead.
Show no fear of rejection by the state
of these men. From, time to time,

to let your fingers bleed.
So the next time you need to have
your prints taken,

the ink will take what you did
for work. Why the officer told you
to hold your palms down.

CORRECTIONS

It's unlikely a doe's standing
frozen between buildings
in a cab's headlights.
Unlikely she weaves herself

through the gridlocked cars.
Looking for a stream, mowed
hay to make a bed of. A fence
to bound over. And not this fence

crowned with barbed wire.
It would take ten deer standing
on each other's shoulders
to reach, the last one likely

to be looking down the barrel
of a CO's gun. To keep her
from bounding over into the yard.
A word hunters use, too.

Where deer huddle in winter,
when they're free to lie down
in the snow. Yet hoping
this winter will be *open,* less harsh.

Although farmers like their fields
covered during the dark months.
So snow will melt into the ground,
raise the grass again. So the men,

behind these walls, will hear the ice-melting-
mountain make a stream and then a river.
For the deer to swim downstate
to the likelihood of the city's harbor.

Taking the Wrong Picture

Not that I wasn't told
ahead of time.
Or hadn't agreed
to the ground rules, the spoken,

written admonitions.
Couldn't guess there are cameras,
like nests, in the nearby trees.
Trained men to report

any wrong doing, innocent
shutter-clicking me.
Who forgets no one is supposed
to be taking pictures on these barred

grounds. Memory being
all I might need.
To remember what I'm seeing—
the walls, the bars,

the towers and men. Inside,
lines and lines of them,
walking one hour
to the next, not allowed to say

anything while they're walking.
It's the rule for what they did.
This line isn't an excuse,
an explanation for the real

deeds that brought them in.
These millions of locked up writers
and readers. A few of them
who signed up for this poetry writing

class, sitting in a half-circle
with me. I have to remember
without any pictures. Their numbers
and their names.

In the Waiting Room

A TV's on. Chained to one
station. As if I'm spending

a night in Motel Seven.
Watching my own show.

And not waiting to go in
through the metal detector.

Escorted. *Silence,* the correction
officer's requirement.

Gate after electric gate.
Until I'm further inside

with them. Those men I've
been cleared to teach, to read

poetry with. The rhymes they found
before I was buzzed in.

Back there in their block,
they call their house. Where no good

news reaches that far into the dark.
I might want to tell them

and can't. Might want to say
what I watched on TV—

the S.W.A.T teams swarming
a French neighborhood, the explosions

and shots, children evacuated.
One boy whose father was telling him

why so many people were weeping,
laying flowers in a street. How a flower

can replace a gun. No matter, even now,
how innocent that sounds. The bell

ringing—didn't we just get here—
the CO's standing by the door.

His job's to clear these rooms,
to make lines of these poetry-writing

men again. To escort me, gate
after gate, to where I came in.

The TV on in the waiting room.
Watching its own episode.

Maximum Security Pen

I agree not to bring in anything
not pre-approved.
To leave my pen locked

in my car. Anything
that can be used
for spare parts.

The poem I write
in my head, thinking it can't live
on a contraband list.

I have to remember to keep
on the tip of my tongue.
That won't be detected,

scanned. A word
inside a word. Spaces
and letters. I like to keep

my word. A promise. A signed
agreement. An understanding.
Until I can't agree anymore.

It'd be dangerous
to hold my tongue. To not
write with anything I can.

A feather. A leaf. A pen
cut out of paper,
dipped in blood.

Sentencing

There's a dance in here, too.
Some of the men lead, some
follow. Say they're in

their dance line. Not
talking. Not allowed
to look ahead

of themselves.
I follow them
through the locked

gates, upstairs to this
steaming, 1930's
classroom.

Where a teacher
forgot to erase a word
one of the men,

my student, wrote over
a year ago. As if it had
more to say to our new

group, this first day
of class.
I'm trying to get more

comfortable, if that's
possible, among them.
The wind beats

on the half-opened,
barred windows.
The crows

on the metal roof, nervous
as high school boys,
checking their dance cards.

Serving Time Stanzas

Let's say I'm allowed to tell you more
than my last name. Which isn't as personal

as the branches losing their November leaves.
They curl, they're wind-swept.

Or write my address on the blackboard,
not afraid someone you know,

on the outside, will arrive at my door.
Asking for anything I can do for you.

Beyond what I say in this cold, overheated
class room, this barred school. Reading

pre-approved poems. The rules of a sestina
and sonnet. What they hold inside

their sentenced lines. I don't want to compare
to the time you've done, the streets

you had to leave behind.
A judge didn't see things

the way you did. We agree you may
write in rhyme or free verse, writing

in your cell I don't have an address for,
I can't just walk to. Even if I had a leaf

with a stick for an escort. If I was allowed
to say goodbye and thank-you.

How Difficult is It?

I wouldn't have guessed
you'd love this form. And take it back
into a cell's darkness.
Even the super moon can't reach you.
Unless you guys dream that light
is meant for you. I mean

it's hard for me to think of so many men,
green-suited, shelves for beds, guessing
if the moonlight
will shine that far back
to you
and the super darkness.

It's darker
than I ever thought. I mean
a moon meant for you.
I never guessed
I'd be inside, this far back
inside a yard's, a wall's dark light.

Locked-in isn't a kind of light.
Although I can think of darkness
as its own light I can take back
home with me. Even if it doesn't mean
I'm here to guess
how it really is for you.

I can't know. I'm not you.
And that shining slice of light
through a cell's window, I want to guess
is the super moon giving up its darkness,
its secret, shining meaning.
So you can find your way back.

All the way back
to this poem's form for you.
So meaningful.
So darkly
full of light.
It won't leave you guessing.

When I'll come back to be with you.
Your guest. A poem turning darkness
into light.

Inmate's Mural

Imagine you have to imagine the sky,
save for the hour in the concrete yard, lifting
weights, talking, planning. Looking up

to the clouds. You're told there's light
behind, a burnt, sienna sunset.
All you see is a sliver of sky,

when you're seeing things right.
So bright you think you're inside,
not quite for the rest of your life.

A day, it's hard to imagine, you'll step outside,
blinded by light. The sun, that coin.
No one will have to cover your eyes.

You'll be so alive. Even if you don't know what
to do next—lift weights, look at the sky,
plan your next step. Imagine how your days

might have felt, if you were allowed
to paint a few clouds on your cell wall,
appearing to pass, night after night.

FINGERPRINTING

The small talk's about Sunday's
Super Bowl. The point spread.
Blackhawks circling the stadium.

Hors d'oeuvres and girlfriends.
Wives and advertisements.
The cost of a scalped ticket.

Hoping the game's better
than last year's. I'm told
to relax my hand. Let the ink

take the prints. Let my thumb
roll without resisting.
A hand wants to grip. Make a fist.

No one's suggesting I make
inside this guarded room.
Save when it's almost Sunday.

And the CO sees
I'm here to volunteer. For the fourth time
to have my prints taken.

To be sent, he assures me,
for our government's review.
To see what demonstrations I

demonstrated in, how many tackles
I made. If it's safe for me
to teach poetry and return.

GATED COMMUNITY

Astonishing how you imagine
that *clang,* beyond the walls,
is a bell, a buoy rocking its waves.

And that shadow, a ghost
of a sailboat warned.
Meant to be following

a channel, drifting, on course.
Amazing how you hear God
in the middle of the night, *clang*

of the CO's gate, his keys,
despair's tympani. And still get up to pee
in what you call your beggar's bowl,

that cup, being what it is.
Its overflowing. An image
your poem isn't meant to avoid.

The reality of where you are.
Where he's banging in your mind,
a boat of blood, your chalked-in-the street boy.

Enrolled

Let's say we're in parochial school.
White blouses, plaid skirts. Boys
in long pants and ties. Rules
to live by. God divided in three
parts—morning, noon and night.

Let's say we're not here,
you in your green jumpsuits,
issued the day you were locked in.
Enrolled isn't the word I'd use.
Although let's think of you and I

this way, for the few hours we have
in this guarded classroom.
To read poems, to write with our blunt
pencils. As if we, student and teacher
alike, could wear anything we could find

in the closet of poetry, to try on, to wear,
even if it takes a lifetime to become
threadbare. Like words, we use again and again,
that don't escape us, that can be inked
in our skin, written on a bar of soap,

passed from cell to cell.
As if they were written by those monks
whose pictures Sister Agnes hung on the wall
in fourth grade. Before we did
anything we couldn't take back.

Teaching Prison

You look at me as if I'm crazy
to want to be inside with you.
Passing a different kind of time.

Serving, a word I never hear you use.
Doing a bit is what you say.
A phrase I could speak, too, wondering

if there's actually anything I have to offer,
to let time pass inside, as if it were
a regular day. Rise and shine, my father

would yell on his way out to work. Before
the sun rose. Before the rest of us
were awake. He never said later.

Short for see you. Not knowing how late,
most nights, he would be.
My sister and I already asleep.

My mother, bottled in, by the snowy
TV. Crazy isn't it, how a poem finds
what it needs to believe? The rules

we can break sitting in this locked
bit of a classroom. Revising the lives
of our drafty lines.

Dear Board

Dear Maybe
Dear Perhaps
Dear Impossible
Parole

Not Changing the Painting

To bring it up to date,
they'd have to hire an artist
who lived nearby or saw photos
from that other, before-now

time. To get the feeling of the first
façade. Before it was decided
the prison needed another wall
in front of it. Twenty feet high.

Crowned with broken glass.
Classic, the way the barred
windows reach toward sky. Light
bulbs shine through, offering, almost,

a holy sense of the lives inside.
The artist felt the feeling of and painted
what looks like a meadow, a lawn.

That may have been mowed the way
he chose to render it. Bright green against
the brick, brown building.
Time lost inside. That inmate

painter painted. Not knowing it would
survive time-served. His and the men today
who pass his painting, in this mausoleum
of its staircase hall. A curator's light

highlighting shades of brown
and green. The facility, inmate to itself.
No one hired to paint in
the concertina wire.

Between Classes

No one's spitting spit balls
in this hall. Or talking.
Everything's against the rules,

except thinking.
Using your mind's
sentencing, the teacher-

in-me wants to say.
Imagining that shadow
on the wall's a crow,

sentenced to his own shrieking,
his own counting, counted
days. The sun setting each night

will erase. When the moon isn't
bright enough to turn a shadow
into a wall's bird. A mural.

Lighting or *alighting*, a Romantic
Period word you learn
you can use, you can take back

to your cell's crib, your nest,
your wire. Where you do
your homework, a year's worth

of assignments. Where, you could say,
you're *assigned* to live for the days
you have left inside. To hear

a crow cawing in the hallway,
the CO's admonishing,
No bird-talking. No wing-flapping.

Your Natural Life

I volunteer to read
your mail.
To circle words.

Report them to
my supervisor's world.
I come to be known

as the Moonlight Reader.
Reading between the lines
for danger's code.

Love could mean *knife*.
Knife a *leaf* on the outside.
I have to remember some words

mean what they say.
Are meant to be felt
by their reader. Sitting

under a maple tree,
in a hall in a walk-up.
Your lover, inside

and out, down the block.
Where a cell is your house.
Where I come to realize

what you're writing
is written for me.
Sitting in the mail room

in the moonlight.
Imagining you, for the life
of me, not wanting to believe

what it was you did.
What got you locked-in here
for the rest of your natural

life. *Natural* a word
I'll have to decide
whether to keep or strike.

If it stands for
the lifetime you have
to write to me.

Lock-up

Before I turn off my light, I've taken
to watching inmates survive night
after night. They pray. They carve paper

knives. They send notes between cells
on fishing line. Thread they strip
from underwear. A CO takes away

what he finds. Steel
poems pumped in the yard.
Years. A mind-serving-time.

A cigarette of air.
Last night I turned to my wife.
I wanted her to read my skin.

An hour of exercise. Regret and no
regret. I wanted her to visit me
to count the days. To love

my penitentiary, my day-dreaming.
Wanted her justice. To watch one
episode with me.

GOOD BEHAVIOR

It's likely the heat's overheating
your cell. So much so you strip
down to your state's pair

of tee shirt and shorts. Plank
as many planks as you can.
It's too cold to go out to the yard,

to sit alone.
You never thought you'd be saying
It's better to stay inside. Barring

the heat shutting off and the temperature
diving. You've written the warden.
And been here so long he's gone

from warden to superintendent.
Two words for the same man.
For that invisible thermostat

he's changing year after year.
Especially, tonight, when you have
to believe there's still a ball

dropping in the freezing square.
Time enough to parole
yourself. To see your breath.

The Poem I am Told Not to Write

because it might say what I hear,
I see inside, construe as a breach,
a compromise.

That could be read as a code, beyond
its surface words. Might be used
as a ladder, a shovel, a pair of paper

wings. A knife or pen, a pen knife.
A chant to memorize and pass,
as the monks did, at night,

from cell to cell. When their abbot
ordered them to sleep, not to be singing
love songs to God, he could only

surmise were meant, each to each,
for a brother at the end of the hall
in the monastery. And not that

consummate Jailer, a strange word
for Love. Locks and keys,
shaved heads and scraped knees.

These men dressed in their issued,
green gowns. I'm not allowed to
write to my students in maximum

security. Now, inside with them,
hearing and seeing. I'm told not
to forget what they committed.

To make a new life from what they can.
With a pencil, blank paper.
With words for their words.

Last Class Poetica

I could thank you for being
with me in this writing
room. For the state

letting me come in.
To read poetry, to listen to
what you've written.

In pencil. Pens forbidden.
Ballpoints use too many parts.
Ink you could tat yourself with,

draw blood.
Signs on your skin meaning
more to you, the men

on your block than me.
Although even a broken
heart, needled on your arm,

speaks to the poems
we're reading. A poet needed
to write, locked into his

feelings. Which, I'm thinking,
is why you have a key stamped
over your heart, you pull up

your shirt, for me to see
as I'm leaving. To remember
you by. Poetry being

a feeling in the body,
in a cell of thoughts.
Words that can find you

later, next year,
month after month.
Where here is your life
sentence inside

this barred building
with all there is
inside.

2

Survivor's Fund

I'm donating a fall
warbler and ten thousand
dollars in honor of my daughter.

Who hasn't forgotten.
Who goes without
saying is singing, years later,

to her daughter. I'm willing,
bequeathing
ten thousand plaques

for the women
who were assaulted.
And their mothers

and fathers, who arrived
on campus
forlorn to be picking up

their daughters.
I'm pledging to look up
the name of that warbler,

the night, the time
and date she returned
to a window, the wind

her shadow. With no more
unnecessary
longing.

CALL AND RESPONSE

You might think it strange to hear
I like to make a sound, somewhere
between a bellow and a moan,

when I'm walking by a field of standing
cows. Letting the note rise from someplace
I didn't know is there inside. I think might

please them to feel we've more in common
than you and I first thought. Call it
desire's stare, their big eyes and numbered

ears, my busy, empty mind. You might think
I'm making more of this than need be.
The practice of emptiness, the image

the Buddha brings. Sitting there,
eyes half-shut, half-open.
Thumb and finger touching enough

to attend to that tender place.
So the mind can empty, the heart fill
with emptiness. Love sounds across this charging

fence. First their moans, then mine. The bellow,
the bull in my throat. The strange thought
there's more to make of our love.

For a Student Attending a Poetry Reading For the First Time

It's hard to tell what you'll hear
as speaking to you. Might assume was written
for a student like you in mind.

Even when the poet, between poems, says
a few words to open the door to the next poem
he's chosen to read.

When he has no way of telling what line,
or pause, might touch anyone, especially you,
in the front row. Taking notes, looking

deeply into your notebook. As if you're sitting
in a 19th century American history class
and it's all you can do to keep up

with the names and places,
the numbers of wounded and dead.
All you can to do to wait to ask

what the poet or, you're learning, a speaker
in a poem intends. When he says
I love you like the snow clinging

to a branch. Whether he's actually speaking
for himself and, in this moment,
to you. When you thought you never

could be anything other than yourself,
reading the calendar of events and doing
what you've never done before. Wandering

into a poetry reading, as if walking,
between buildings, head down to save
yourself from the driving snow. To not

have it appear you're going to a room,
a laboratory in the science center.
Where, you had read, a poet would be reading

his own poems in honor of International
Women's Day. In his own written voice.
Where, you didn't know you were hoping,

you'd be seen in this century's moment,
experimenting with a new sense of yourself—
isn't that one of the reasons to go to college—

not taking history notes. But beginning to
write your first poem in the margin.
Thinking of words as leaves buried in snow.

SEE SOMETHING, SAY SOMETHING

My neighbor says, in passing, he's feeling
the shift of fall to winter. In his body.
Says, it's hunting deer that gets him through

the season. In fact, he adds, some of the geese
are trapped inside their clouds and wishes
he could pry them out. I know him well enough

to know he's not kidding. But not so well
as to ask him more without him thinking
I was prying. Stepping beyond our friendly

neighborhood. Privacy sometimes a cloud
for what someone's really thinking.
Maybe I should call his wife. Or ask him

point blank, I'd rather say directly, how disturbed
he's feeling. Offer to walk over to his house
beyond the trees, down his long driveway.

Anytime he hears the geese calling him.
And it might take two of us to talk them down,
to release them, to where it is they're flying.

Old Man in the Mountain

Our parents drove us to New Hampshire
to see the bear dance on a rope.
We were old enough to cheer for the bear

but not the rope. I wanted to stay in
the car to see the Old Man in the Mountain.
Afraid of men dressed up as bears.

But not of stone faces. Father said
if we looked long enough, we'd see a man
who could become president. Up there,

where the bears slept, they weren't chained
to a trainer. Where an avalanche,
I learned later, moved the stone into a profile

of a lost, elected face. We would drive all the way
from Boston, to see the shadows changing
his expression. Over time, the rocks needed

braces to hold what they could in place.
Driving home, breaking their long day
of silence, father would look at mother

through their front-seat smoke. As if to say
something barely meant for me and you, my sister.
Words the bear spoke for the mountain.

AFTER HEARING ALBERTO WAS PULLED OVER
BY OUR TOWN POLICEMAN

for driving a few miles over
the speed limit. For not knowing
what a row of blue lights

meant for him to do. And following
him into the Marriot parking lot.
The cop sitting in his squad car,

then walking over to him.
To ask about this time's flashing
moment. The driver-in-me wants to

think how often we have another
chance to offer ourselves to one
another. In this case, for the officer,

a young man, to hear the accent
in Alberto's speech, and, I want
to hope, to hear it

as one of his own notes.
Nothing to question further.
Nothing for which to ask him

to step out of his rented car.
To separate him from his vehicle.
Cold words for a spring night.

For two men to take a chance
to listen to reason.
For being here inside

each other's story.
Alberto's tells us later.
There are times we need a visitor,

who isn't a stranger, to show us
how we're living in our town's
detaining village.

WITHOUT SPEAKING

By looking. By coaxing.
Occasionally imploring.

One of us is all
   imagining. The other
touching. Imagination's

best becoming.
   Not a moment given
to remembering.

Thoughtful now
   and now again.
Nothing left out

or saved for later.
   Everything made
in the love-making.

Hive Mind-Synching

My friend, sitting outside a café
on the Left Bank, texts me she thinks
our country has lost its collective
mind. She puts down her phone
to watch the cabs and buses,

the workers walking over Pont Neuf.
I've been there once
which is enough to write
its name. And not feel I have
to text her back to defend

my life. Still living here
in the country, a half-mile
from my town's temporary polling
station. A word to tease her with,
taking a selfie standing near

an electric fence, a small herd of Polled
Herefords, curious enough to amble
closer, to see what the reflection
of themselves is about. To see
if I have a handful of grain

to feed them. Not that a handful
would add to their weight-in-the-world.
Would do anything more than delay their
turning away. For less time than it takes her
to message me to do anything

one person can do. To see inside a thousand
backpacks and briefcases walking by her.
To know what she doesn't,
she wouldn't have any way of knowing.
She could use the hive mind of her friends,

her Facebook friends. A corporate name,
a stanza ago, I was reluctant to use.
Until one of you posted for both of us
to look up from our phones. To see that
package synching at your feet.

Lascaux's Gym

Perhaps I shouldn't say anything
    about that horse inked on your back.
The lines you had drawn there.

Burned. Traced
    from a cave. In France.
Maybe I should keep my thoughts

to myself. Where, it appears,
    we're here to work-out. Not think
suddenly of that man,

that woman and their horse.
    Shadows on a wall.
Where stone is skin.

Blood is paint. I want
    to believe you cared
about the pain.

What the needles made.
    And the beautiful way
your horse roams

across your shoulder blades.
    When you lift weights.
And I'm not afraid

to ask, what that horse means,
    if anything. If it was meant
to be seen in daylight.

By someone nearby.
    If it's there to take you
away in time. If, looking again,

it's a body without a name
    that only appears to be a horse.
You paid, you bled for.

In a cave. If anything I say
    can be taken the right way
at face value.

Tracking Forgiveness

Stevens wrote "The Imperfect is
our Paradise." Some days paradise is all
we have. A sentence

to live by. A therapist says
we're allowed to make twelve mistakes
a day. What's forgiveness for,

if not to set our watches by?
I wear Christ on my wrist
and have a hard time believing

everything Stevens wrote.
Remember he was an underwriter
who wrote poems and insurance

policies. I want to make as many mistakes
as I can in my lifetime.
So I can be my own actuary, sign

Perfection's policy. My wife says
I shouldn't have left the bird feeder out
for a bear to trash last night,

to leave his tracks in the hungry snow.
Says she married me so we can live
in paradise.

Moonlight and Hammer

"...those men and women/Brave, setting up signals
across vast distances..." —Muriel Reykeyser

Your name on a building doesn't mean
anything to me or the clouds.
Pigeons aren't meant to read letters.

No one needs to know how much
you were paid for a building to use
your name. Below, the street could care

less and below that. My country
used to be a country, before it became
a brand. And never one, branded nation.

A cow on a ranch. A fraternity brother.
A posed Apache, Native American logo.
No American is born polite and politically correct.

First, we're outspoken. At first breath.
Selling your name comes later.
Selling yourself short isn't the same

as being sold down the river.
Above, I was speaking of you and not myself.
A street can become a river. Under a sign.

Who came later was assigned a name.
I wish my last name was River.
Syllables that flow together, further

than one my family was given.
In the old country, we had names
from nature and work we did.

Moonlight and hammer.
Red-wing and cobbler.
Our mayor was a stay-at-home father

and mother. Where all good work
was done in nature.
No one thought to weld

her name to a cloud.
To read who was president.
A song the red-wing sang

rose as the letter of the law.
As far as our government went,
it goes without saying.

I've Made it a Habit of Waking Up

and walking in the morning.
Letting rain and snow, the falling
temperature, begin each day

with their own predictable
surprises. Overnight bobcat
tracks. A coat, frost-heavy,

draped over a mailbox.
The sense everything and nothing's
the same, going out, coming back.

Particularly the invisible wild
turkeys, who seem to make
a point of leaving a semblance

of themselves in a few feathers
released as signs on the road.
Where, it appears, they unknowingly

point a way into the woods.
As if you and I can make as much
as we need to of their absence.

Of flying without flying.
Hiding in the empty branches.
Not to make a poem

of this image too quickly.
The turkeys a tree protects
from the wind. From the memory

of a neighbor dreaming in his forest.
Another image, I'm not sure
a poem is ready to save.

Ready to save a second way of saying
ready to keep. To write down and, one
morning, eventually, to type.

MOTHER AND FATHER

asleep in their pulled-
together twin beds.
The TV still on,

watching itself, a re-run.
A white stallion rearing.
A masked man.

A sidekick Comanche.
The televised fake rocks.
Silver bullets to leave

behind. To show who was
there. I was coming in
late again,

wanting to say *Good night.*
Not surprised I found them,
in their own beds, side-by-side

in Nineteen-Fifty-Nine.
Ash glowing
in the ashtray.

A diamond
with fire inside
I thought, approaching

them. Trying not to
shake Rossini's telling
overture, the strings'

tumbleweed, the horns,
the arresting tympani.
Flutes and piccolos,

arrows above them.
The words I didn't say,
each night.

I didn't want them to know
it was midnight. It was me
turning their screen to snow.

To Your Perpetrator

I'd mail him a valentine
of knives, if I knew
where he lived. A box

of heart-shaped
snakes. I'd be his UPS
man, deliver chocolate

nails and napalm lace.
An unsigned card
of threats, greeting him

each time his doorbell
rang. I'd burn a ring
of cinnamon around his

perpetrating house. Dare him
to mow his grass, I'd plant
with IED's, a father's home-

made, tripped device. I'd
devise for him for his
deliverance. Tripping

all over me.
I'd be so in his face.
Eye to eye. Tooth to tooth.

Love being the place I'd bite into.
No Christ of red
forgiveness.

Inside and Below

It's hard for you to see the sun
reflecting off Kim's giant windows,
without thinking he's still

alive. Most likely you didn't
know him. Unless there's a man
in your life, larger-than-life.

Whose hands are bale-sized.
When he looks at you
you find the sun

inside his eyes. Wild turkeys
and deer browsing late
in the afternoon at the edge

of his field. Snow coming,
he would say you can tell
by how the crows alarm

themselves. How breath
gathers into frost
on a window. So you can

build a fire and watch the glaze
mist. You, meaning all
of us in Kim's giant world,

inside and below.
Where the sun goes to hold
a mirror.

For the moment you see
yourself in the eye
of a window. Those deer bounding

away, turkeys winnowing
the hay in one
of his furrows.

Heaven

That first night it's likely you won't be able
to sleep. More like renting a room in a motel
and trying to guess what a sound means

in the next room. If she's kept against
her will. If the occupant forgot to turn off
his TV. Here sound's an eternity

of gasps and moans. Of making as much
as you can of a rented bed. And having
to decide to call 911, to have the stars

break down a door. To see what's happening.
Even when it's too early to think
in familiar terms. On night one.

When you haven't put away your things yet.
When no one knows where you are.
For whose sake. Or if you're where

you thought you'd be.
Trying to fall asleep. Hoping to read
that blinking No Vacancy sign.

Not Making More of Where I Am

My love, I'm climbing
into the ditch,
to pick this random

spray of daffodils.
A bride's tossed-away
bouquet

Bulbs rising,
half-buried. At least,
if I'm not mistaken,

what the wind raises.
So I can step, ankle-deep,
in spring's come-to-be

run-off. Snow melting
in this side-of-the road
garden. Love's centerpiece

on a ditch's table.
I'll leave here for another
morning. Threads of hay.

A bottle thrown one night
when a boy, driving mad,
thought no one was looking,

no one would hear.
What his girlfriend said
to drive him crazy.

Still in love.
What I'm here to leave
alone. This spray of spring's

yellow, flowering
microphones.
Not meant for me to think

of taking the sun's
offering.
Not making more

of where I am
inside your love-
making.

CONSTITUTION

When I bump into my friend Steve this morning,
he doesn't hesitate to tell me he and his new wife will
enjoy a late breakfast at The Bridge in Addison, Vermont

near Lake Champlain. Enjoy the names
on the plastic menu, for battles and one fish
resembling the story of the native Vermonter

whose line became tangled in an endless
monster. Whose tale is told whenever the ferry's
crossing. This morning after their Ethan Allen

omelet and Redcoat coffee. Steve says he and his
bride will walk over the water by way of the new
bridge spanning the story. Tying two states

together over The Narrows. Where the dead
can be counted. Shipwrecks and drowned
flags. Where a fish appears to be a monster

to any couple out walking celebrating a first
long marriage and this one, Steve says will
last as long as there's a Revolutionary name

for eggs and bacon, pancakes and sausage,
onions and peppers, home fries and reenacted
maple syrup, a cook calls The Constitution.

Ending the Rumor

Shelf-stocker, fruit-stacker, meat-cutter,
sandwich-maker, bread-deliverer, mostly
women-at-the-registers, after-hours-floor

sweeper, beer men, carton cutters, teenage
part-time workers, past and present
owners, behind-the-deli glass caterers

catering to their neighbors, to passing-
through travelers, middle-of-the-night
truck drivers, here, by the train's stopping,

the engineer leaving his Vermont
Railway engine idling, running in
for what-used-to-be free coffee, his saved

newspaper, some early morning talking.
Call it conversation and not about
the store-closing.

Empty as Now

Call it a chute instead of a gate,
this gray, steel-barred, one cow
cage. Empty as now one waiting

for it. Coming and going.
Not knowing if heaven's
on the other side.

The chained bed
of a loading truck. A field
flowering hay. Urging

and prodding. Say a cow's
dumb as a new day.
When it's us who wake up

not knowing how we'll be used
for what. If we'll fit into
that portable, temporary cage.

Driven to the next field
further away. To a licensed,
hanging-by-weight house.

3

Calendar of Leaves

November's a leafless feeling.
Don't think there isn't anyone
who hasn't felt this. Say
grief's a universal, selfish feeling.

Whoever said any month is a month
for grieving wasn't kidding. Was plain
speaking. Knew how numb
you could feel as the year turns

over its new leaf, making impossible
promises to keep. I was foolish
to think you'd live beyond your
keeping. Long life doesn't promise

anything. A new month. A moon
feeling like a calendar
of leaves,
a page of branches.

Assisted Living

I would have wanted a nicer view
for you. Instead of this wall, outside
your door, raised to mute

the road. To keep
the coyotes at bay. Wanted a bird-
of-paradise to split the concrete.

So you could see its latest blossoming.
Even the flower doesn't know why
it's here. For whom

it was meant to be. Only that it rises
beyond itself. Beyond any desire.
Useless now, for me to think

you could've used more space,
for more than a dresser and a bed,
two chairs for visitors. One

or none at all. Save for the night
nurse who'll need to get off
her feet. Who will sit there for me,

the miles between us
what they are. Too much time
and space. A universe of shining

regret. All that I have to remember
tonight. The hall between
our rooms. The train across

the road we couldn't see.
Peonies bursting
against the house.

THE LAST TIME WE DIDN'T TALK

I was sitting by your bed, watching you
move your lips. I could see there was

a breeze high in the palm leaves.
As if the leaves were speaking for you.
As if the freeway, beyond your door,

said what you would say.
If a few words could rise
in your throat, make their way

beyond your mouth.
I had to imagine with my heart
what it was you might have been

saying to me, what a sister would
say to her brother, the whispers of leaves
shaking each other. Below the clouds

opening, leaving room for a sentence
of sky to write itself across both of
our minds. Our thoughts, racing

and still. Too fast, I want to say now,
when the only thing left is what
we might have said in your going.

The silence we'll keep to ourselves.
And the palm trees swaying.
All that noise jamming the freeways.

LOWERING YOU

It's possible you're listening,
as they lower you into the ground
to our mother. Even this far
away, I have to imagine you still
make quite a pair. Your bouffant

coiffed hair. Eyes-lined,
looking into death's instant camera.
The Polaroid, that died
its own death, giving way
to a new model of itself. That,

so quickly, shows you yourself.
Looking up, listening to the words,
the grave men have found a way
for me to say what I can. My words
crumbling, as they lower you down

to her. One of their phones, they
use as a speaker, tied to a string,
that's held over you. So I have
to believe you both might hear
the prayer I'm speaking on speaker

phone. Words our father, buried
over there by the freeway's drone,
would have to unplug his ears
to hear. If only he could still
listen. To any echoing word.

APPARENTLY

they think the black
dirt is the wrong color.
The men who dig a home

for you. So they cover it
with a green rug, a swatch
of Astroturf. So bright

it isn't grass at all.
Which leads me to
believe, they don't want me

to grieve ahead of time.
Before I have to leave. Having
thrown a fistful of dirt

into a square, a well
dug hole. After I'm gone
they'll fill in by hand, a shovel

being a hand's machine
and God's. Where, nearby,
they'll lean themselves against

the nearest tree. Having done
their work for me. Folding a flag
of grass to rest in the back

of their custom-made,
scaled-down truck. The one
that fits between graves.

Later they'll wash what they call
their bright, burial cloth.
They don't really believe is meant to

shield me from what I have to see. The real
mound of dirt and stones, beneath
that piece of shiny lawn.

THIS EARLY

Maybe you're waiting for me
to speak first. To speak to

the wind who knows where
you are in this first week

of your leaving. Even if writing
leaving implies one of us knows

where you're going. The snow appears
to let go of its knowing, riding

trails of the wind's invisible
tracking. Where we've been isn't

where we're going exactly.
Neither of us has to

to speak first. We can leave
to the wind to know that for us.

Maybe I'm saying all there is
to be said in writing, the space

between words and surrounding.
Maybe I can read the snow falling

and rising, as the trail of our in-between
silence. The wind filling in

nothing we have to know
this early.

A Poet Wrote the Moon

Some candles last
no more than a week.
Flame and flicker in

their glass bowls.
So when you walk by the candle
lit in your house, you'll remember

how long a week is and short.
How a room's shadows come
to stand for her. Your sister

who isn't here in her own body.
Who waxes and wanes, the moon
in a bowl. Before going

to bed, you might think
to rest her in your kitchen
sink. To know where she is

when you're sleeping. Of course
I mean the candle
losing itself, its light disappearing.

A poet wrote the moon
is a heartless memory. Rising
and setting. The poet

who didn't have a sister
to see through
his window.

4

Please Don't Thank Me

for the three months
I served, stateside, in barracks
more like a dorm than a hooch.

When my friends were overseas,
sleeping in rain and blood. For more
than a year. Some of them returned

to less than a canteen of thanks.
A few said, *Don't feel guilty.*
What good would that do?

Even if I remember the base
I trained on in San Antonio.
The burned and grafted taking

their morning walks.
Grateful to be there and not in
a thankless paddy. A Huey

chopping the air, taking too long
to land. To lift them. Past
please and *thank-you.* Words

we were taught to save us.
I can't thank you enough for not
thanking me for my service.

I'm Not the Best One to Ask

why we make stones
from words.
Why we forget who we are.

What we mean
to each other,
lying beneath the stars.

Can't say how night comes,
night after night, leaving us
speechless. Afraid

to say stone words
we're meaning to ask
of the stars. What it takes

to be taken away
from ourselves. To clear
our throats of stones.

To be the best one to ask.
Isn't a star a stone? Never
alone exactly. Never one

to say what it means to be
lost. In the space between
words. In the pause.

Rue de Vivre

Recalling the café's sidewalk table
on the *rue*. People-watching people

walking by. The train from De Gaulle.
Gang-graffiti walls. Designer poverty

galore. Kicked-in doors.
Tickets to the Louvre.

Therapists sunning by the Seine.
Their patients pay them to say

*Don't take this personally, madame et
monsieur. Life's this way. Even yours.*

Recalling the traveling you did
to feel you lived to take

words personally.
To see that pregnant woman

hanging by her hands on the cement
ledge. The wounded and dead

inside. The man who drew her
back in, to have her baby indoors

she'll recall on his birthday.
The table and the tourist who hid

under it. The terrorists, *mon Dieu,*
who came to this and not why.

Love Beyond Us and the Falling

Perhaps our love can save the memory
of our government. The night we remember
to lie in the grass and even the voles aren't afraid
to vote for us and not one of their own.

Aren't trapped, running in circles not meant
for them. We promise not to forget the thought
of each other and the feeling of happiness.
Even when the field changes its mind

and we believe it instead of ourselves.
We're two grains in a granary. Small
and vast. And willing to undress in sight
of the sun. To make love anywhere

there's a chance of victory. Of taking
ourselves into account. Of laying down
our lives for an empty flag. Remembering
how long we can survive without

touching, believing in love beyond us
and the falling stars. Beyond thinking
there's another election inside
your eyes and mine.

Taking the Weather Personally

How kind of him to scoop salt
with his hands and spread it,

whenever he sees a sidewalk's pond
of ice. Whenever he believes he's told

to do whatever he can for all
of us, in his world of our town.

How he hears God, each morning,
telling him there's no diagnosis to keep him

from casting kindness from a pail
spilling salt and sand.

His Galilee. His personal rink
on his daily walk. True, isn't it, we, too,

can take the weather so personally we think
we're losing our minds? That God

has it in for us. When really God's whispering
to do anything we can to help

the ice melt, to put treads
on our shoes. To keep from slipping.

Although isn't that what we need, too?
To be less sure of ourselves.

On the Lift

There's not a better place
on earth than sitting
with Bill McKibben

in County Tire's waiting room.
Our cars hoisted on lifts.
Two men behind

the glass, swapping out
sets of tires. Balancing them
with weights from fishing

lines, the balance
bubbles showing our wait's
almost over. Although

with the clouds gathering,
the temperature dropping,
it may be better to pray

the snow's staying away
for one more swapped day.
To let the plows stay

where they are
in the town shed.
Salt and sand rising

into a mountain again.
The roads clear and no
black ice, no freaky snow storm,

we could have predicted.
I don't have to say anything
more about to Bill.

How we go about saving
the earth, one season-to-the next,
winter-to-spring tires.

Downton's Last Lawn

With four episodes left, the writer
leaves it to us to guess who Lady
Mary will let fall in love with her.
A former lover? A man, a woman still
to be uncovered? Perhaps the groomed

lawn, nature being the lover
that it is. Foreshadowed in Season
Three, when Mary, leaning in,
seemed to kiss the water
in the fountain. Saw her own,

another's rippling reflection.
Leaving us to see it wasn't just sex
she was after, after all her survived
disasters. Wasn't putting love
ahead of running the class-crumbling

manor. Or gender. A word not
invented yet for them. Although there's
really no confusion as to what the men do
and the women. Although the writer knows
her history to write into a script's changes.

To leave it to us to guess who, what Lady
Mary will end up with. Loneliness, a camera
panning over Downton Abbey? You and I
not knowing what we'll have to do now
on Sunday evenings.

Using the Right Words

My father sat me down
to talk sex, a speech I'd never
heard before. I told myself

to gaze out the den's window.
Through Brookline's maple leaves.
Over Karp's roof. All the way

to the Green Line's T. To train me
to the MFA. Although I'd rather say
trolley, given the painting I'd find

in the American collection. Childe
Hassam's "Boston Common
at Twilight." Two girls feeding

pigeons next to their mother.
The gas lights coming on,
Men in their business hats

a few steps behind.
And the natural, glowing light.
I learned rose from a fire

beyond the leafless trees. Closer,
if I have the true direction,
to where we lived. When I wasn't listening

to my father, all business that night,
trying to use the right words. Not
for the street and streetcars,

that mother holding the younger girl's hands,
the scattered seed, the birds pecking at
the shadows and the light.

How We Come to This

When I see you I speak
a language I never learned
to speak. Close to the bobolinks
spilling their songs in the hay

fields. They used to sing
when there were enough hay stalks
to nest in. Leaving me speechless
with you, lying where we can't be

seen. Listening to the field-
singing-field. First love, time
and time again. When I see you
I've no words for on the tip

of my tongue. Touched and not
touching. Feeling beyond
words. Beneath the signs we make
with our speaking hands.

The sign for lips. For tongue.
The sign for not knowing how
we come to this, my love,
my fountain.

Not Refusing Them

I could call that boy,
in his father's arms at the prow
of the raft, a head-scarfed

Odysseus. Say the wrong word
for what they are doing.
Not *disembarking*.

But jumping, knee-deep,
into the thrashing Lesbos sea.
The island, one stone to step on,

to take them where they're going.
Too many of them
for that boat to carry.

Its maximum number erased.
And who's taking their lifetime
of money. So they can live in a tented,

permanent shelter, speak
a new language.
His father's holding a sign

Poet and plumber.
Hoping he'll be discovered,
they'll be waved onto a ship

in German. They can walk off
and not into deportation's
water.

Searching for the Pope in Pomfret

A girl will usually answer
when you call
a Vermont general store.

When you need to know an address,
the best road to take
to arrive at a stone.

The dates carved in, a name.
Even the love he came for,
if you can imagine what's written

in the earth below the stone.
Where some love is buried
and spoken. You don't know

if you should step out of your car
to walk closer. To where he strolled.
With her, his companion

philosopher. Not lovers, we're told.
Although the apples, each fall, left
over, say something other

than what hasn't been said.
The passion in letters, in what goes
unspoken. Papal clothes

not worn here, next to the river.
A cross he left in the woods
for the woods to bear.

Call it a souvenir, undiscovered.
A girl who works in the store
never heard of when you call.

To ask if there's a sign
you should look for
to know he was here.

Visiting Poet

No one told me I'd be sitting
across the table from Deyanira, number
two wife of Hercules, the name her parents

assigned her. Sitting in her classroom
at the foot of Grass Mountain,
a dry Olympus. Where the gods

wear masks of spiders and snakes,
the dead drum their Chumash bones.
No one gave me a heads up, across the road

fans still drive to the gates
of Neverland. To leave notes to his
ghost, love's allegations.

Everything that he did here.
Isn't a poem where we name what was done?
Where a goddess can be saved

by a god from rape? Blood's
a river, even in this drought.
I want to assign you a line you can

dream, then write.
Bring to class tomorrow
when I'm gone. Imagine you were

named for a goddess like Deyanira,
gazing out the window. Thinking
of that boy across the road

writing his note to Michael,
hat-tilted, one-gloved, dancing
his moon walk.

Next to the 101 in Santa Barbara

No one built a fence around that giant
field. No owner, no government.
No workers kept out, stopped

from stooping over,
hand-filling crates and pails.
Even with those monster machines

harvesting all they can
in the moment it takes not to see
them, migrating one row

to the next. Because, it appears,
it's better to sweat here than south
of the border. Mail money home

across the river. Near two
presidents' graves in the vineyards
of California. Once theirs.

All their ancestors wanted.
Rabbits and wild horses,
their own fences. Hope being where

they sang, picked grapes
and oranges when they wanted.
Where they could welcome strangers.

And there were no Pick-All-You-Can signs
for us gringos driving through,
wondering where they went

when they were done picking.
Where they slipped home to
in the moonlight.

Returning to the Counseling Center

It doesn't take long to remember you
once worked here. Listened to Redwings

singing, scratching their throats. Reading
the body language of branches. And later

writing your clinical notes. Diagnostic
codes for a swan who didn't want

to leave her room.
The wind who knew he was a girl

who couldn't be coded. It's hard to forget
you sat by a window looking out

toward the mountains. Its shades
of light, its seasons of faces. Whenever

you, too, felt discouraged. Not knowing
when listening makes a difference or how

long it takes for a swan to step out
of her room, a girl to forsake the wind.

There are many stories of branches,
professional and personal notes. To leave,

to take with you. To fill in the spaces.
To recall the widening circles

of water, those students who were
patient with you.

COMING ACROSS IT

Such a beautiful distraction
    spun through a thousand
mouths. More visible now
    the leaves are down.

That wasp's bag is
    not quite gone.
There's always two left
    to spin love's colony.

To guard their grey globe's
    emptiness,
Call them love's probes,
    their stinging tongues.

Say you didn't see anything
    behind the left-over leaves.
Wouldn't you like to go on
    and not stay here wondering?

Until the snow comes. Not
    to undo any beautiful thing.
Until there's still this one—frost-
    winged, dazed and stumbling.

Submitting Poems to the Local Paper

So Bev Megyesi can stop me at the counter
to say, Gary, I didn't know you were a hunter,
having read my poem in the local paper,

the one the editor chose. Because it coincides
with the last two weeks in November.
Overlaps with the speaker's voice in the poem.

Which I tell Bev is my poetry-speaking voice, the one inside
my head I write on paper. That's news to me, she says.
It sounds so much like you I thought you were

a native hunter and the deer in the fourth
stanza was one, a flatlander, like you, was too shy
to admit killing. Dragging from the bloody woods.

I don't know how to thank her for thinking
I've lived here long enough to sound like a rifle shot,
a buck huffing his last breath. There's almost no

difference between the speaker in the poem
and the writer sitting in his room, the woods
for readers and poets. Isn't it the almost

that counts a lot? So readers like Bev and you
can see yourselves holding a pen and a rifle,
walking across a written field. Wanting to make

sure those points you see are antlers, before
you raise your gun, write anything down
for your neighbor to read in the paper.

ADVICE

Experts say we're likely
to think terrible thoughts between
two and four in the morning.

Terror a form of worrying.
Worrying a step above fretting.
Fretting wanted more than not feeling.

We usually feel better
in the morning.
Fear having more to do

with a body's temperature
rising. Than how
we carry day-into-evening.

Worry, trying to fit into a bed
made up for dreaming.
What if this theory's wrong

I'm thinking?
Trying to remember
if I was sleeping, if I was too cold

without knowing it?
If everything I thought was true
and not fleeting.

Even when my wife's shaking
me, saying not to believe what
I'm dreaming, I think

needs to be written.
Sun flooding the window.
October's mercury falling.

5

Posting Poems on Facebook

Thank-you, friend, for your *like*
to the poem I posted yesterday, posing
the question of what you might do,

if you came across a club, apparently
abandoned, leaning against an elm.
The putter standing for anything

you might need, you found.
Left there to be taken away
with the trash,

or, perhaps, for a friend who knew
his neighbor was moving,
discarding what he wouldn't need

in his next life. Thank-you for
commenting on the name of
the club's maker, "Odyssey"

and how, for better or worse,
I invoke the word's myth.
Although each time I slip off

the sleeve of my putter,
it's as if I'm sailing with Ulysses,
my map the drawing of the greens

on the back of a scorecard.
My way, an unrecorded score.
Penelope waits with her men

back at the clubhouse. Even if, friend,
you feel I'm going too far
by naming the club, the name, too,

of Homer's caddy. I thought these days
could be ascribed with an ancient name.
Doesn't a poem have to risk as much as it can,

know there aren't meanings for every dream?
And you'll have to decide what you'd like
to take home and if it was meant for you.

AT THE CHURCH OF OUR LADY OF TEARS

Who are they? I don't want to know.
I want to see.

JAMES WRIGHT

Maybe we can read the sign
together, one language
at a time.

Translate enough words
to make one sentence
between us.

Maybe Sister will stop
texting
long enough

to bless us and
and the marble
dust, weeping

beneath our feet.
And Virgin Mary
will cry through

her plaster
eyes.
For Antonina,

pregnant Antonina,
to enter her
sainthood

for what she saw.
For what, my love,
we're not here to see

exactly.
For the Christ
she is still seeing.

BASIC TRAINING, 1972

I was trained to breathe in
a training room.

Ordered to lift my mask
to taste the gas, let it burn.

To feel how it feels
to cough up blood.

I was told when to get down
on all fours. Which way was out.

Through what door.
Outside, the sergeant said.

And what I could do with my tears,
the burning air.

Unbuttoning the Sky

Stars mean to come down
the first morning
they hear geese dotting the air.

Alarming isn't it?
What their migrating line does.
How the stars want to align.

Buttons on a black blouse.
Stones thrown to the ground.
Leaves of another kind.

They're not here for us
and go by going
where they are.

Wing's thread. Most mornings
we're not meant to connect
the dots. By looking up.

Setting off love's alarm.
Most mornings there's nothing
they can say for us.

It's all they can do to read
the stars. To make a bed
of the field.

Some mornings
we unbutton the sky, before
we leave for work.

ICELAND'S GRIMSSON

Our president refuses to admit
what's incumbent of him.

He's buried a glacier of diamonds
on an offshore island.

How fortunate for him.
We fill Austurvollur Square

outside parliament.
Throw yogurt and fish.

Rise like steam from the Blue Lagoon.
That spa for taxing tourists, American

and Japanese. We protest
for as long as it takes for him to turn

red in the face.
Our tax-evading president.

See our reflections
in a sheet of ice.

Surround ourselves
with syllables of sheep.

Names a volcano can pronounce.
Once we were all myth and kings.

We didn't have to crowd in a fishy square.
Shout at a window for him to appear,

provide fresh towels on request.
The Hotel Borg, across the way,

not our residence. Here in Reykjavik.
Words are bones

to stick in your throat. Songs to call
Grimmson out.

LISTENING TO WAZIR MARIA TOORPAKAY ON "FRESH AIR"

Most likely a tuft
of deer tail
snagged on the barbed fence.
A few threads left.
A cloud wisp. A trail

of smoke's another
guess.
A ghost. As strange
as a *telltale*, a sport's
term,

by the side
of the road.
Did you hear what
Maria Toorpakay,
the Pakistani champion

squash player,
that Wazir girl, said
on "Fresh Air"
to Terri Gross?
Her father, singing

his banned poems,
told the villagers,
the dead were better
listeners than them.
His daughter, quicker

than a white-tailed deer
bounding over a fence
in a four-walled court.
I'm adding here for her sake
and the sake of his poems.

Her life of changing
into boy's clothes,
so she could play
the game she loved.
Using her body how

and where she chose.
Choosing what
a deer doesn't know it's doing
for us. Fleeing, fence-jumping.
Its kind of playing. Listening

to Maria describe
the disguises she wore
to compete. To be the girl
with a quick stroke. Anywhere
on the world's court.

THE MONK'S TAKING PICTURES

of what he's made, this sand
painting in the lobby
of our library. We're standing,
waiting for what he'll make

of his million colored grains.
One of Buddha's sun designs.
He'll sweep into his hand,
to let prayers sift back

into Compassion's vase.
I think I'm here
to browse, to take out a book,
this Sunday afternoon.

And not to walk by
and stop. To want
to hold what he's holding
in the meantime. This invisible

hour glass. When a woman
nearby asks if he feels sad
letting go of what he makes—
all that beautiful mind.

He doesn't quite say *No.*
Says, instead. *It's natural, like death.*
Dismantling what
it takes to free this kind

of making. What I find
myself doing as quietly
as I can, taking a picture, too,
for another time.

Welcoming You to the Counseling Center

I would be anxious, too, calling
for the first time, walking through
a third floor door. An attic of sorts
in the college's closed fraternity house.
Open now, fittingly refitted, for its view.

I can tell you it was Donna
who lobbied to have us work up here.
So when you arrive, you'll find her
welcoming you to the Green Mountains.
Not a picture outside, but the mountains

themselves, behind her reception desk.
Beauty to remind you of your beautiful
worry and the sun rising, beyond
your dormitory window. Even
when it loses itself for a while, behind

a bank of clouds. Donna can see, too.
Sees how the clouds have come
over you. And yet how talking
to her before your new
counselor walks from

her office to greet you.
To have her introduce you
can make it seem as if you were friends.
As if you were home.
And talking could help you make friends

with yourself again. Helps your clouds
disappear. Truly, we wouldn't have been
here, if Donna, on the day we were about
to move, from one building to the next, didn't
put her foot down and say

we couldn't listen in the basement
of a fraternity house. Its keg-tapped ghosts.
Its six packs of college boys. Said we needed
to work on the third floor.
Closer to the clouds and sky.

Easter's Ginsberg and Corso

"I moved ahead, eager to rejoin old company...
I went to the movie of my life," —Ginsberg

I'm reminded this day before Christ
rose, Gregory Corso invited my friend,
Peter, and me, to drive him to Ginsberg's

and Orlovsky's farm, down state,
for Allen's birthday. Peter lived in a commune
with Gregory in Buffalo.

Where that poet was loving his Methadone
and heroin. Two lines in his high
poem. The one he promised he'd write

on the drive down. If only we could
see our way past what we'd find.
Men sitting around a dining room

table, waiting for Gregory to arrive,
rise with them. Once, Allen began playing
his harmonium, breathing life with his feet

into its canvas lungs. Raising his voice,
no one would call singing, really.
If you weren't stoned on love,

men's love. Peter and I—am I remembering
right—espoused in the abstract. Seeking
advice, in those days, from the I Ching,

those pictographs of sticks and stones,
their random messaging. Should we stay,
should we go? Wondering if we could stand

listening to our back seat poet, droning
for hours on the Thruway. Driving
our crystal Christ, wearing a shawl

and his court jester shoes, their tips curled.
Gregory said Allen would have him
take off at the door. Said Peter and I could leave

our clothes on, when the dancing began.
When, he wanted us to know,
there'd be more than one Christ

rising, coming down. Even if we left
the car running all weekend, by the private
gate. If we'd be there to drive him home.

Bookstore Reading at Gibson's

Why not have Brother Sylvan, the bard, appear,
  bearded and staved, in the front row?
Rising in his monk's robe.
  Don't we need a priest, a man, tall-

as-a-pine, in New Hampshire,
  to sing a poem's way
to survive our century's plague?
  It's easy to assume we've outlived

the Angel of Death. Poetry keeps us immune
  from nothing in this Concord bookstore's
nook. We don't listen in order to concur.
  To know what occurred in a cold

cell in another time's place. When one killing could
  lead to another. When a germ could escape itself.
When we were one ocean, one continent.
  And all it takes now is to open a book

not on the Internet. On a shelf instead.
  And a few chairs and a microphone.
A bard. And us stepping out
  from the amplified, assembled woods.

Pancakes and Kabobs

Our town invites three thousand refugees.
We used to count ourselves in, our town
of nine hundred fifty-three. We'll have to

rent extra seats for them to raise their hands
at town meeting. Roll out blankets
to kneel and pray on.

Some of us are more fearful than afraid
of pocket bread, head scarfs, and smoked
lamb's tongue. Some of us speak

two languages in our sleep of field and sea.
Where they're from they rarely vote
by closing their eyes, resting their heads

on school desks, raising
their hands, like we do.
When we're concerned

what our neighbor might think,
we write an *x* for *yes* on a piece of paper,
y for *no* or leave it blank

as an open field. When we're asked
to vote on how many new citizens
we can take in. Remembering an empty manger,

a boat teeming with fish, that first nurse
who welcomed each of us into this swaddled
world. Before we knew how to pray we'd be

wanted here. Sitting or kneeling.
A skull cap under a baseball hat. A blessed
silk scarf to give away. Or wear on a cold day

in March. The parking lot overflowing
at our polling place. The folding tables covered
with pancakes and kabobs.

NOVEMBER STREET

These geese can't tell
where they're going one field
to the next, looking for wheel-
ruts and cornstalks, a wet place

to spend the night.
The moon having risen,
the stars fallen.
Telling, isn't it, how even

they can't navigate
without one of them leading,
sensing there's a field
to land on, enough to eat

amidst their honking?
Which we could say is like
some of us living one
paycheck to the next. Praying

a sidewalk walker will stop
to read a sign.
I'm hungry. Will do any work.
Will fight again for our country.

The stars and stripes.
Praying one of us will reach
down to lift him, as if
we were a government,

and told we have more
than enough. And not to worry.
Tomorrow that light in the sky
is the sun.

Retiring, really?

He says he's retiring at the end
of the year. A year's a season.
He's so well-seasoned, Boston's
Dominican. Swinging for the fences.

Where a fence is a wall
monster. Some nights he's all
smiles. Some days he bares
his teeth. This bear

of a Dominican.
We'll be lost without his swing.
I don't want to think of him
kicking back, polishing his bling.

Although he deserves everything
coming to him. A wind
blowing out to left. A designated,
lifetime fan. I like to think of myself

as one of his record-breaking, going,
going, gone statistics. Almost Spanish-
speaking. Spitting into the palms
of my gloved hands. Stepping

into a chalked, dirt box. And
with one flip of my bat—
call it his wand, *su varita*—
it's gone again, leaving the park,

that ball driven from the big man,
retiring itself for the two us.
Let's retire his number
but not his name. And that

breeze blowing out
to right, to Ortiz's bullpen.
Who said, after the bombing,
This is our fucking city.

Are You a Poet or an End?

Who would you be in the moment
   the ball's tipped into your sudden hands?
When you've been coached to leave thinking

   behind, practiced those given routes.
When suddenly is what the game's about.
   And your hands, soft

 as a retriever's mouth. Isn't an end
   whistled-trained not to bring back a ball.
To take it, an announcer says, *to the house.*

   A zone you'd like to live in at the end
of a game. Surprising yourself at what hours,
   late in the afternoon, can come to.

When you were tired of what
   you had to do like a machine,
on command. Run out. Cut right. Trust

   the ball will be there. On time.
Love what you'll find in your hands.
   Love the safety who made a mistake.

BUS AND SUBWAY

Like you, I used to ride
the bus and subway

downtown to the Commons,
some nights to a gym the mayor called

our Garden. One day to Logan Airport
to stand by a metal fence

to watch the planes glide in. Over the harbor.
So close I could touch a wing.

I never told my father where I'd been.
Even now, with him approaching 96, I'd know

he'd worry, listening to his console radio.
Believing he once heard God announcing

the camps are free. The Jews were fed
and bussed to nearby cities, however far away

they were. Eventually train-boarded. Flown home.
Home, an orphanage,

a family who would take them in.
I can't help remembering, seeing

Brussels' men and women, the children wandering
the streets, the dead lying in their blood.

What's happening here again. The trains running,
station-to-station, underground.

Good Energy in the Room

Between the turbine and the trees,
wind churns the leaves into waves.
My poetry mind wants to convert

everything into darkness
and light. Singing and whining.
A single blade's song. I don't want

to make up my mind yet, if it's good
or bad—that wing on the hill slicing
the light. Piercing a good night's sleep.

Shaking the blinds. The stand-up
comic-in-me wants to step up
to the mic and start my set turning

off the lights, using my voice
instead of the microphone.
What's a poet for if not wind-spinning,

standing in front of a good night club
crowd? For a moment, not knowing
if what he's about to say will turn

the wind into the sun and the sea.
Without using up a word.
If he feels good energy in the room.

And still sees a patron crawling toward
the door. By the candle of her cell phone.
Back into the windblown, leafy street.

Walking Out of the World

Someone will have to tell the bridge
we're standing on, when it's time for us
to return to school. To break

our seventeen-minute silence,
imitating the silence of the dead.
The river will have to recall itself

for what it is. A river flowing
behind a school. We were told never
to ferry ourselves across it, to trust our bodies

were rafts. To the underworld.
Let the traffic be what it has always been.
Curiosity-seekers slowing to read

a sign, seeing who may have survived
their own wreck. And men and women
with guns in their gun racks, fighting

the urge. On their way to retrieve
their children. Having earlier dragged
a shanty from the melting ice, spooled

their reels, in order to look
forward to another season sliding
a fish house onto the ice. Not having

to defend their right to stay up
all night watching a hole
in the lake. For a shadow to rise

back into this half of the world.
Part of a story we're missing
by virtue of standing here. Over

the sleet-soaked river. Below us,
that raft of leaves, someone thought
to set on fire.

Vetting a Vice President

My children like to say their mother sleeps
one heartbeat away, next to their resident
father. If he were impeached,

she'd roll over to be their president.
They like to say at the foot of the bed
lies their third-in-line canine,

barker-of-the-house. Although
when he barks, he speaks for them
and not succession. Although to be

First Pet, waking up howling
allegiance, wouldn't be
the worst scenario. To place

his paw on a bible. To lick
the Chief Justice. To be hailed
by my children as their heart-beating,

surrogate father. Who didn't know
he was leaving. Each time
he rolled over, away from their mother.

None of the Above

Perhaps it's not what you say
about how the starlings,

without thinking, veer as one.
Maybe I misunderstand your tone,

your voice, a thousand starlings
striking their chord in the deaf

pines. So they might think they have
to repeat themselves, dawn after

dawn, to be understood. To feel
they have choices, even when one

of them signals the nine hundred
and ninety-nine others, it's time

to veer. To pick this branch or that.
To light for a while among the answers

leaves provide. Or, perhaps, to pick
e., none of the above, the letter you choose

when you're as sure as you can be
of uncertainty, the sky inhabiting

this flurry of birds. Who have a thousand
ways of turning into one. A choice

the wind doesn't know it can offer,
ask you to understand on your own.

April 8, 1974

after Rossin's portrait of Hank Aaron

Isn't there something about taking your own
picture of his painting, his open-collared
shirt, his winning smile? As if he was rounding

third base again, heading for home plate.
His teammates waiting to greet him.
Ruth's record broken. The hate mail time-

frozen. Something about holding your own
camera, standing in front of him.
As if you're speaking to each other in this color

portrait. Seeing things in black and white.
Although it's hard not to forget
a White boy broke out of the stands, to run

the bases with him, thinking he belonged
there, the ball rocketing over the fence,
record-breaking. Not taking into account

what he was stealing. As you might think
I'm doing, too, picture-taking.
Although there isn't a guard

walking toward me, raising her hand,
telling me to put away my camera.
And not to stand in front of this gallery

displaying rendition, remembering
to hear the cheering fans,
the shutter clicking.

Remembering Today

My wife invites herself into my back room,
to organize the lives of my books.
She's not afraid to say how uncomfortable

she's feels not knowing where everything is.
Where she can expect to find what's there.
I tell her I have a general sense

of where things are, having touched each life.
So I think I know where it is.
She says that isn't good enough for her

and hopes she still has for me.
Having the best intentions,
when we first met in the library stacks.

Downtown, in Buffalo, beneath
a steel plant's smoke.
When our friends and we thought

more promising thoughts of what America
could be, how it was possible to read
and march, put our bodies where

the police didn't want them to be.
To shut down a street. To stop the war
in its paddy tracks. To fall in love,

sitting on those library steps, holding
a *Hell No* sign. I won't think to say this
Valentine's Day. When she's in love's

overflowing room, rearranging everything
to her and, she hopes, my liking.
By theme and writer. By if it looks like

the book was ever read.
By the likelihood, someday,
I'd ever want her to give it away.

Shading the Doorway

"Dieneces answered "If the Medes darken the sun,
we shall have our fight in the shade."
—Herodotus, *The Histories*

What's the difference between a president
sitting in his situation room or his den,
watching a broadcast in real time

of our enemy taken out?
His advisors leaning in, their expressions
astonishing. As if they didn't believe

what was happening on the screen.
Inside Bin Laden's lead-walled room.
Or the one upstairs where he could've

easily have been. Watching a movie
before heading to bed. Into what he calls
his tossing and turning room. Seeing

the bodies of lost service men. Their
families sitting around the box
of their television set, a screen screwed

flat to a wall. A folded flag it'll take
a lifetime to accept in real time.
Herodotus, writing his histories of war,

stepped outside to see what he had
to record. The bent shields.
Couriers between villages.

The bleeding fields.
Before he could return to his tent
to write what he saw. Leaving what he felt

to a blind poet. To recall what she dreamt.
The differences between men and women.
Not to become too polemic about this.

The difference between a war room
and a tent, a bedroom upstairs. Where
everything and nothing gets said.

The enemy's dead. "We got him.
Isn't that his wife and children,
shading the doorway?"

It's Easy to Love You
When You're Not Here

and the leaves are.
Easier still to feel
love's empty branches.

When there isn't a word
between us.
And the sky's full

emptiness.
We're all we are
and the sparkling

grasses.
We have to work
at this. And isn't work

overrated.
Difficulty's retired
prayer. Love

in the love-making.
Making more
of less. And better.

RESTORATION

I'm writing a new protocol to hold
    the Middle Ages at bay.
Isn't there something to be said

for cold chambers and big fireplaces?
    For an Internet that hasn't been
invented yet.

I'm writing a set of new guidelines to restore
    the Renaissance.
Even when it's hard to keep up

with who patronized whom, what painting went
    with which painter.
And why anyone would want to paint

on his back, drinking celestial drippings.
    Why a man would want to sail
to the ends of the earth.

Only to return with stories
    no one would believe.
Return with fleas, infecting anyone

who didn't want to wash
    his hands.
Who didn't believe it was God speaking

into Shakespeare's ear.
    Couldn't imagine a time other than
his own.

When a word would have to be
   saved for what caused grave after
grave.

When the living would be asked
   to sit at a long table with feathers
in their hands, bowls of ink.

With all the time in the world
   to write what rules
they could.

Opening Day

The plows are out,
sanders spreading
salt. I'm sitting

next to my radio
listening to last year's
broadcast. With all

the other shut-ins.
A phrase I'm too old
not to use. Although

I don't want to give
the impression I'm not
able to sit in the stands

watching April's crocusing
snow. Seeing the tracks
a grounds crew makes.

Although I see, too, a line
of deer prints, the split
hooves, how quickly they can

disappear. The plow's
blade attempting to clear
the ground. So this spring's team

can slide and slip out
of the dugout. These Spanish,
and Japanese, these American men.

Rabbits really, when they
steal bases, catch their fur
on fences. Even our ponderous

designated, hitters. We're promised,
at the start of a season, are here
to make it home.

Like bears lumbering back to their dens.
A promise, I'm making
to myself, to see them as men

not bears, to listen to my radio. Inside
in my bleacher chair, loving, my dear
New Englanders, our snow delay.

Once in a Blue Century

The Chicago Mounted Police prance
their steeds outside the bars
on Clark Street. To keep
everyone in. These delirious citizens.

Their team having won the world
championship. For the first time
in this century. Who knows what
to think watching a horse drink

beer, down a few shots. His rider
trained to look the other way, once
in a blue century. No one knew
a street could become a rodeo

of happy drunks. Having another one
for the sake of their thirsty Lake
Michigan. Ivy guards Wrigley's
outfield walls. Where a ball can get

lost in its own excitement.
A walk-off home run. A horse
running around the bases. Touching
all the bags. Toasting

a pink elephant, a phrase saved
for another circumstance.
When a stadium becomes its own drunk
tank. The mayor charging the police

to mount their horses. A poem might
call a steed. To keep even the sober
sitting in their seats. Until ecstasy dies
down. The pennant is raised.

LIVING IN THE SIXTEENTH CENTURY TODAY

after T.R. Hummer

The vendor stores his wagon
   somewhere. Why not here?
Leaves his vest and felt hat
   on a hook. Say next to his car

inside the parking garage
   next to the park.
Let's say he's learned to throw
   a bag of nuts as far as he can

with an accent. Taught his monkey
   to make change. To flirt
with your destiny. Even when
   you didn't know you're sitting

on a bench the team's owner
   wants you to believe is a chair.
And not a throne in a street
   in Verona. Men in pantaloons,

concessioners in rags. Shouting
   as if they were singing,
Signora, Signora,
   fresh peanuts here.

Chagall's Girl

I'm assigned to sit next to the new girl
from Iraq, to teach her elementary school
English. I didn't ask to volunteer to point

to things and say their words.
It's Nineteen Fifty-Four again.
There are names for things I can

point to, in and out of school.
My friends look at me as if I'm
the traitor I am. I begin to like her

sooner. Holding her hand on the yellow
paper. I can tell she thinks three letters
make a bird, this girl from her former

land. She asks me if I know
the word for magic. Showing me
her wings at recess under her blouse.

My friends don't understand. Threaten
to never speak to me again.
I'm too young not to believe in

threats and *Shorbat Rumman,*
her mother's pomegranate soup,
she brings for me in her *thermos.*

That *chalice* holding hot and cold.
Two words I didn't know I knew.
Until she rose as if she were one

of Chagall's girls, rising over
her hometown, smoking village.
As if those curling leaves

were notes. And not her father
yelling to her from the parking lot. Not
my friends, taunting her their love.

BREAKING-IN

The police call to say they think
    there's been a break-in.
My father wakes me to say we have to drive
    downtown. Tells me to grab
a hammer in our basement.

Says this is what glass means.
    In Boston. In the Combat Zone.
Where police run their own protection
    racquet. Guaranteed, as long as business
men, my father, pays them off.

Leaves them Yuletide checks. Even when we
    never light a tree. Pray to one, eight-candled,
God instead. When we arrive, the sergeant's smoking
    in his squad car. We walk past
the first door's scattered glass,

unlock the inside, second one, intact,
    (we don't say) as our one God. My father doesn't
pay his precinct dues.
    The sergeant didn't have to say that.
In Nineteen Fifty-Three it's clear

what the rules are. How much should
    have to be paid to him to raise a glass
on his Christ's birthday. And never to forget,
    the windows shattering
on Boston's *Kristalnacht.*

SPRING ICE

Judy's daffodils droop under
the weight of our managing,
top-down government. Supposedly,

with the sun out, they're supposed
to spring back by noon. Announce
themselves again. Forget how

ice lobbies them to bend-
to-almost breaking. Freeze
in place, as if they never blossomed,

showed their button-holing faces.
In the Rotunda's lobby. Where everything
for and against takes place in an icy,

three martini lunch. Junkets
to a distant island. A room free
for the afternoon. A key. Flowers

in glass vases. Judy's my planting
neighbor. Her bulbs are vote-
resistant. They wave their blossoms

when they need her. When spring resists
itself. We vote with pen and paper.
We cast our names in yellow.

Completing Their Service

No flower-sniffing bull
pasture-bound.
No Derby's thoroughbred,

stall-held, meant to spend
himself studding.
No tent-less domestic

retiring. This herd
parade, a tide
of elephants.

These ancient, unpaid
serviced girls. Packing
it in. Sent to Florida's

preserve for pachyderms.
To remember who they were.
Hind legs-standing. Trunk-

holding a spangled girl.
Flag tail-grasping and waving.
Trainer cane-led. Around

a sawdust circle.
Call it a ring. Their Barnum
and Bailey, Ringling Brothers

world. Call it anything
it isn't. Their free-ranging
savannah, greatest place

on earth. Where, we've heard,
they mourn for us
for trucking them

in trailers. Letting them out
to run around
in dust-disturbing circles.

In Auschwitz

Leave everything where it is.
The stones, the dirt, the chimney
ghosts. Nothing's there

for you to take home.
There's a law against this
and morning's guarded mist.

Don't allow yourself to think
work will *macht* you free,
when all there is

is feeling beyond
the barbed-wire,
branchless trees.

The earth calling you to fall
to your knees. To actually
be there, for the first time

in your mind again. A prayer,
a poem, no one's
last word.

Leave yourself completely
unprepared. The bus
idling in the parking lot.

Only so much time
saved to walk under
the wrought iron

gate. To let a palm-full
of ash—a bird's, a leaf's,
yours and theirs—sift through

MUSEUM OF ISLANDS

At my age, my friends say I'd better get out
and travel when I can, before time
takes its toll at the toll gate. Before the last

national park is closed. And the airlines stop
letting me pre-board. Sit closer
to a World War II pilot, who's close

to giving up his wings. Landing
a few minutes ahead of time.
Friends tell me to attack

my bucket list. A map of places that want
to see me before I forget where to go.
The sun shimmering a river. A mom

and pop store, off the road, known
for its early morning cider donuts.
And early morning. When, lying in bed,

I can forget how old I am, scroll through
pictures of where my friends have been.
The museum of islands. A palace

of rented rooms. A rock overlooking
a sea, they say, hasn't been named yet
and is waiting for me. To book a reservation

with all the miles I haven't frequented.
To step out my front door with my right
foot, my father assured me would keep me

safe. Whenever I thought I was going away.
Whenever he said not to worry,
when he didn't return on time.

ABOUT THE AUTHOR

GARY MARGOLIS is Emeritus Executive Director of College Mental Health Services and Associate Professor of English and American Literatures (part-time) at Middlebury College. He was a Robert Frost and Arthur Vining Davis Fellow and has taught at the University of Tennessee, Vermont and Bread Loaf, and Green Mountain Writers' Conferences.

His third book, *Fire in the Orchard* was nominated for the 2002 Pulitzer Prize in Poetry, as well as *Raking the Winter Leaves: New and Selected Poems* (2013). His poem, "The Interview" was featured on National Public Radio's *The Story* and Boston's ABC Channel 5 interviewed him on the Middlebury campus reading his poem, "Winning the Lunar Eclipse," after the 2004 World Series.

Dr. Margolis was awarded the first Sam Dietzel Award for Mental Health Practice in Vermont by the Clinical Psychology Department of Saint Michaels' College and the Covey Community Award of the Counseling Service of Addison County.

His clinical articles have appeared in the *Journal of American College Health Association, Adolescence, The Ladies Home Journal, Runner's World Magazine* and he has been interviewed on his work with college students by *Time Magazine, ABC* and *CBS News.*

Recent work includes a memoir, *Seeing the Songs: A Poet's Journey to the Shamans in Ecuador* and *Runner Without a Number,* a book of poems.

Time Inside was typeset in Minion. In designing Minion font, Robert Slimbach was inspired by the timeless beauty of the fonts of the late Renaissance. Minion was created primarily as a traditional text font but adapts well to today's digital technology, presenting the richness of the late baroque forms within modern text formats. This clear, balanced font is suitable for almost any use. The inspiration for Slimbach's design came from late Renaissance period classic typefaces in the old serif style. The Renaissance period was noted for its elegant and attractive typefaces that were also highly readable. The name Minion is derived from the traditional classification and naming of typeface sizes, minion being a size in between brevier and nonpareil. It approximates to a modern 7 point lettering size. The Minion design's lowercase characters use old-style glyphs in keeping with its Baroque typeface roots. These are most noticeable on the lowercase "g" and "q". Subtle, but important, details allow the upper and lower case to match well and sit comfortably next to each other. The letter "z" in both cases has the tell-tale heavy dropped serif and matching line thicknesses. The strokes of the upper and lower case "y", with its italicized narrowing of the secondary stroke, reinforce the strength of the primary stroke. Interestingly, the "Z" character has a thick stroke in perpendicularity to the "Y", and though it may look a little odd on close examination, within a body of text it enhances readability by providing good differentiation between adjacent letters. The overall appearance of the Minion design is very much related to the appearance of mass-produced publications of late Renaissance but there is an added touch of classic typography design not possible with older, inaccurate print machinery. This new take on those old styles has produced a crisper outline. The Minion typeface family has been expertly crafted to retain great readability by producing a print clarity that even the best of the Renaissance typographers could not manage.

DESIGN BY DEDE CUMMINGS
Brattleboro, Vermont